A

Table of Contents

Introduction

My name is Aaron C. Padgett Jr. You are about to read a collection of children's poems that I have written over the years. I started off writing small sentences about how I was feeling at the time. As the years moved along, my writing improved. My father submitted some of my poems into contests. A few of them have been accepted and published. My pop told me I should continue to write for children like me. There are adults who write children's poems but none of them can speak from a child's point of view. "The World As I See It" is children's poetry, written by a child poet. I write about struggles in school, problems at home, and the journey to become better at whatever sport I am playing. I am the brains and my father is the muscle. I write my poems and he works to get other people to see them. He says it is something we can do together while I am young and still want to spend time with him.

The ideal reader for this book is someone nine years old and up. I write about things that are currently happening in my life. If your child thinks they are the one that has drama in their life, you will like this. If you have a crush on a girl and do not know how to express it, this is for you. If you have problems in your family, it is for you. If you want to tell someone how much they have hurt you, this book is for you. If you are an athlete and have that burning desire to win, it is definitely for you. If you see funny things happening around you all the time, you will enjoy this collection of poems.

If there is one thing I would change about my collection of children's poems, I would have included more. Besides writing poems, I had to complete hours of homework, study for state exams, train for Brazilian Jiu-Jitsu competitions, participate in weekend basketball programs, try to learn some Española, and spend time with my family. I will include the new poems I complete to this collection. Most of the poems are short and under twenty lines. This means it will be extremely easy to read on your computer, tablet, and smart-phone. Thank you for downloading my poetry. Please take the time to write a review. The feedback will help me improve my writing skills. If you connected with any of the poems in an emotion way, please share the link so others may do the same. Thank You!

Return to Table of Contents

Dedication

I wanted to say thank you and dedicate this book of poetry to all the people that have helped me throughout my life:

To Steven for being the best big brother possible

To my brother Najee, one day I will beat you in basketball

To my baby sis Danielle, I love you and think of you always

To Auntie KiKi for making every Thanks Giving special

To my cousins CJ, Tahlik, and Kahlil; every time we are together we have lots of fun

To Big CJ for being in my life since I was two

To Mrs. Maia, there is too much to thank you for so I will just say I appreciate it all

To my first group of friends, Dylan, Janae, and Jaylin; we pushing ten years together

To my Godmother Velicia, thank you for all the weekend get-aways

To my God-brother Daniel, we will have many memories in the future

Thank you Aunt Linda for all the love (Mama T. R.I.P)

To the teachers and staff at Icahn Charter School IV for not giving up on me

To Evelyn, Tyler, Sydney, and Sadie for adding something special to my life

To my Grand Ma for the daily love. Grand Pa, do you remember wrestling in the hallway

To my Dad, you are a pain most of the time but I know you are pushing me to be my best

Return to Table of Contents

School Bus Anxiety

Every day on the school bus I hear yelling, screaming, and hollering all around me.

I see paper airplanes, spit balls, and girls staring at me.

I can't blame them I am hot, but when the bus jumps I go plop.

Then the girls laugh and I say stop.

You see children getting in trouble for no reason.

The bus aides become guards and they act like you committed treason.

Kids are laughing, having fun, because they telling jokes about yo mama.

One child starts crying and it's all because a few kids started the drama.

Mothers running on the bus screaming at the kids to leave their child alone,

Kids reaching in their pockets to video tape it on their phone.

But when I get to school everything's alright,

When we see the principal we all try to stay out of sight.

Return to Table of Contents

A Life Without You

A life without you isn't a life.

The thrill of loving again is no more without you.

I need you making my life better every second.

Your smile is enough to light the world ten-fold.

Your beautiful hair makes silk jealous.

Your personality beautifies the very world we live in.

You are the electricity that fires my soul.

Return to Table of Contents

Christmas Letter To Santa

Santa Claus I know I been a little naughty but can you give a kid a second chance?

You don't know the whole story because I look at the world with a different glance.

Making a good choice every day is the really hard part,

But if I could get a few gifts it would be a good start.

Maybe a microphone or a guitar so I can hang out with my friends and be a star,

Maybe a bike so I could go far and do tricks on the handle bar.

I just want a second chance to get my niceness back,

I know there are kids who behaved better than me and you may not have time for that.

I just want you to know I have seen the errors of my ways,

And I will be good for all my future Christmas days.

Return to Table of Contents

Journey To My Camo Belt

The Journey To My Camo The Obstacles In My Way,

It's Like The First Day Of Training Was Yesterday,

Triangles Double-Legs Armbars Sweeps These Are Some Of The Techniques,

I've Trained And Trained And Finally Have The Strength To Compete,

Brazilian Jiu-Jitsu Is The Martial Art,

White Belt Is Where We All Start,

The Camouflage Belt Is The Highest Ranking,

When I Reach It I Still Have To Continue My Training,

Rolling With The Lions You'll Get Ripped Limb From Limb,

The Training You Get From The Gym Teaches You How To Win,

When We Are On The Mat You Can Hear The Speakers Rumble,

The Friendship The Struggle The Life Lessons We Learn In The Jungle,

I Was Taught That Bushido Is The Warriors Way,

I'll Take These Lessons And Use Them In Real Life Every Day.

Return to Table of Contents

All Because I Missed The Bus

Missing the bus is so annoying, I run then trip and I start falling.

I see some friends that are in the same position, when they tell me their stories I had to listen.

When they are done I run to school, while I run I feel like a fool.

When I get to school I feel relieved that I can learn and leave.

I try hard to follow directions but when I try to explain the teachers will not listen.

They misunderstood, my intentions were good but I still get sent to detention.

When I walk home I feel like that was total madness, missing the bus created all this sadness.

Return to Table of Contents

I Loved You

I can't help loving you so much. Calling you all the time just isn't enough.

I remember your smile. I haven't seen you in a while.

All I have to say is…

        I loved you, I missed you, and every single day I thought of your name.

        I loved you, I missed you, and every single day I never felt the same.

The way you left me in the dust, the memories we had just wasn't enough.

It's like you forgot about me, I was history and you went on your own journey.

I feel like I was deserted and when you left I was hurting.

        I loved you, I missed you, and every single day I thought of your name.

        I loved you, I missed you, and every single day I never felt the same.

It's like you left no love. It's like you just said good bye.

You I could never trust. I look at you in disgust.

Back then I was always crying but now I'm always flying.

You better be ashamed of yourself, thinking about you and no one else.

Return to Table of Contents

Friend or Foe

When you need them the most a friend has your back.

A foe hurts you and tries to make you crack.

A friend talks to you when no one else will.

Even when you try to be nice, foes mock you still.

A friend is someone that you can trust.

When foes say they are your friend they lie because they must.

A friend is someone who can help you grow.

If the guy wasn't mean I wouldn't call him a foe.

A friend doesn't treat you like dirt.

The foe is ugly and calls you a squirt.

With your friends you can share your feelings that are deep.

The foe manipulates your feelings and his apologies are cheap.

When nobody else will, a friend plays with you.

A foe is a coward and has to come with a crew.

So ask yourself, Friend or Foe, which one are you?

Return to Table of Contents

I Feel Left Out

I feel left out, I feel alone,

I need some warmth but there is no sun,

I walk alone in the dark.

The cold wind is in my way.

I try to move but the snow says stay.

I see different families having fun.

I talk to neighbors and wish someone would call me son.

Return to Table of Contents

A Loyal Companion

Walking you, feeding you, singing to you and more,

 feel like hugging you when you roll on the floor.

 speak my feeling to you every chance I get.

When I bathe you, you wiggle, then we start to giggle, and then we both get wet.

A loyal companion is what you are. When I need help you are never too far.

But there is not enough room in the apartment for you to live.

And right now I do not have any money to give.

So what I want is only a dream.

I wish my parents said you could be with me.

Return to Table of Contents

Through Every Sin

You always acted like you didn't care and when I asked why all you had was a blank stare.

So you ran away and every day I regretted that you chose not to stay.

I wanted to be loved by you but you don't show your feelings and it kills me every day.

I hope one day you make better decisions and finally learn how to listen.

I truly miss all the things that we use to do, and I really don't want to be without you.

I needed someone like you to go through this world with me. There are so many adventures out there for us to see.

My dream is for it to be me and you through thick and thin, with love we can make this work through every sin.

Return to Table of Contents

Broken Heart

feel like I'm losing you. It is like we see things differently.

do my best but it never ever seems to work. It is like you keep pushing me away.

eing with you used to feel like Christmas Day.

st to see the smile on your face made me happy.

ow I feel alone, there is no more comfort from you. I see a lot of things going on.

o you think I'm a fool? You are coming here and going back, I don't understand.

m so confused because I don't know who you will choose.

he thought of you leaving is tearing me apart. I love you enough to let you be free.

ıst go and make something of your life without me.

Return to Table of Contents

The 100ᵗʰ Day of School

My first day here was scary and new. I didn't know the kids names, I didn't know what to do. I kept forgetting my teacher's name, could you tell me again. I feel like I'm starving, lunch is when?

Hooray, Hooray, it's the 100ᵗʰ Day
We celebrate this time in a special way,
We go to school every day and we are here to stay,
We've learned a lot and you can't take it away

I can tell time, a quarter past, a quarter to. I understand the food cycle and all the things water can do, I now know my teachers love and care for me, I feel like I can fly, I know the best is in me,

Hooray, Hooray, it's the 100ᵗʰ Day
We celebrate this time in a special way,
We go to school every day and we are here to stay,
We've learned a lot and you can't take it away

Now at recess we all know each other's name. We have a lot of fun when we play a game. I'm no longer scared to raise my hand. I can't wait to graduate and take a stand.

Hooray, Hooray, it's the 100ᵗʰ Day
We celebrate this time in a special way,
We go to school every day and we are here to stay,
We've learned a lot and you can't take it away

Return to Table of Contents

A Message To All The Teachers That I Can't Stand

Teachers stay spitting in someone's face while yelling

At us because we got in trouble during recess.

They can never tell a good joke when we are good in class

I can't stand when they make you write 100 times

"I will not draw on my tests."

Teachers try to be your friend after they yell

At you because you disrupted the class.

I know they do all of these things in order to

Make us smarter and a better people.

I now see that it is foolish to draw on your test

Because your work is a reflection of yourself.

All the things teachers ask us to do can be very hard.

I understand that these things are not that hard in comparison

To how hard the real world can be

I thank them for yelling, hollering, telling bad jokes, and

Giving me hard assignments because it has given me an opportunity

To prove myself. To prove that I am as bright as everyone says

I CAN BE. PUTTING ME ON A PATH TO DO EXTRAORDINARY THINGS.

Return to Table of Contents

Spicy & Fresh

She is spicy she is fresh

She is cool and nothing less

She got that fire in her heart

She likes to fight with lots of spark

She is so beautiful it's a crime

She really doesn't know that she is a dime

When she sings, it's like a siren's song

Best believe I am where she belongs

Return to Table of Contents

River of Despair

Sitting at the river of despair,

Crying to your reflection and wishing you were there.

All the bad memories I wish you could erase,

You are the source of the pain on my face.

Still I cry at the river of despair, but then I stop crying aloud,

Laugh to keep from crying,

And accept that you must not care.

Return to Table of Contents

Flower Pedals

Love is soft and nice,

Hate is rough and full of spikes,

Love is like a flower,

Pick off the pedals and it will break apart,

Let's try not to pick off the pedals so people can remain in love.

Return to Table of Contents

Watch Me Go Hard In The Paint

Driving down the court,

Fighting through the crowd,

Going to the paint,

Trying to draw the foul,

Got the easy foul and the other player thought it was a crime,

Got my two free throws trying not to cross the line,

Going down the court is so easy it's a gift,

Next thing you know it's dribble, dribble, cross, and swish!

Return to Table of Contents

P.R.O.M.

P is for the paralyzing crush I had on a girl in my class...

R is for the random idea to ask this girl out...

O is for the only girl I had my eye on for so long...

M is for the many years we will spend our lives together...

Return to Table of Contents

A Message To NiNi

Your Little Boy Is Going To Grow To Be Strong,

His Life is Going To Be Really Long,

He Is Going To Be A King,

He Might Want To Sing,

He Is Going To Be The Real Thing,

Now I'm Saying Thank You For Being There For Me Since I was Three,

You Never Took Your Eye Off Of Me,

You Keep Fighting So You Can Prevail,

Because You Were Not Meant To Fail,

You'll Be Successful That Is My Guess,

You'll Bring Your Baby Joy And Nothing Less.

Return to Table of Contents

Thank You All

The times we shared the love we had,

How angry you were when I was being bad.

All the memories we have together,

And the constant help to make me better.

The chicken soup when I had the flu,

And for all that I have to say THANK YOU.

Return to Table of Contents

Made in United States
Troutdale, OR
01/05/2024

16698119R00015